Tyne & Wear

Edited by Donna Samworth

Contents

The Poems

Tall Tales

I saw a little fairy
I saw her at the fair
Then when she looked at me
She got a terrible scare

No you didn't, you didn't
I did

I saw a red monster
I saw him in the air
When I looked at him
He pulled off his hair

No you didn't, you didn't
I did.

Ellis Ferguson (7)
Ashley Primary School

Tall Tales

I saw a magic dancing fairy,
She was right next to a pond,
I heard a screeching noise,
It was her with her magic wand.

No you didn't, you didn't.
I did.

I saw a big green monster,
He was very, very hairy,
I saw him in the fish shop
And he was with a magic fairy.

No you didn't, you didn't.
I did.

Erin Abdulla (8)
Ashley Primary School

Tall Tales

I saw a big green monster
With little eyes and a crown
I saw him outside our school gate
He was very dark brown

No you didn't, you didn't
I did

I saw a beautiful unicorn
With a magical horn
I saw her at the bus stop
That's where she was born

No you didn't, you didn't
I did.

Cameron Hamilton (7)
Ashley Primary School

Tall Tales

I saw a white dancing unicorn
She had a beautiful purple mane
She was running, running faster
Down the winding lane

No you didn't, you didn't
I did

I heard a sparkly fairy
With some lovely purple wings
I heard her in the meadow
See how lovely she sings

No you didn't, you didn't
I did.

Jessica Trotter (8)
Ashley Primary School

Tall Tales

I saw some bright pink unicorns,
With gorgeous dark red manes,
I saw them at the bakers
Clopping down the lanes.

No you didn't, you didn't.
I did.

I saw a pretty pink fairy,
She had a small and shiny wand,
She was prancing around the flowers,
Next to the blue duck pond.

No you didn't, you didn't.
I did.

Sarah Ferriday (8)
Ashley Primary School

Tall Tales

I saw a bright pink unicorn
She was running down the lane,
She was sitting in her pyjamas
And she had a very long mane.

No you didn't, you didn't.
I did.

I saw a gorgeous, pretty fairy
She was flying very high,
I saw her in my sparkly garden
And she was flying in the sky.

No, you didn't, you didn't.
I did.

Sophie Richardson (7)
Ashley Primary School

Tall Tales

I saw a light green fairy
She was holding out her wand,
I saw her with a fishing rod
She was sitting by a pond.

No you didn't, you didn't.
I did.

I saw a giant brown monster
He was very, very hairy,
I saw him in a fish shop
He was with a magic fairy.

No you didn't, you didn't.
I did.

Craig McDonald (7)
Ashley Primary School

Tall Tales

I saw a hungry mermaid
Sitting on a rock,
I saw her wave her shiny tail
She had lost her sock.

No you didn't, you didn't.
I did.

I saw a scary ghost
Sitting on the roof,
I saw him in a spooky park
He was going *woof.*

No you didn't, you didn't.
I did.

Demi Roberts (7)
Ashley Primary School

Tall Tales

I saw a cute, nice, pretty fairy
With a lovely starry dress,
She was at the seaside with her friends
They were really making a great mess.

No you didn't, you didn't.
I did.

I saw a nice pale unicorn
With bright skin that was pink,
She was in the park next to a tree
It really made me think.

No you didn't, you didn't.
I did.

Anja Chow (8)
Ashley Primary School

Tall Tales

I saw an alien with one eye
He was dancing round the fair,
He went to get some candyfloss
It got tangled in his hair.

No you didn't, you didn't.
I did.

I saw a colourful fairy
She was playing at the beach,
Her wand was twinkling in the water
Then the little fairy had a peach.

No you didn't, you didn't.
I did.

Jade Lovely (7)
Ashley Primary School

Colours Of The Rainbow

Red is the sun setting on the sea
Orange are the flames of a bright, burning bonfire
Yellow are the tall, bright street lights shining in the dark
Green are the trees swaying gently in the breeze
Blue is the sea and the waves crashing down onto the rough sand
Purple is the colour of sweet-smelling violets.

Amy Punton (11)
Burnopfield Primary School

A Roller-Coaster Journey

When you get on it you might get a fright
But you can't get off it before it starts to roar and move
When you go up a hill with a chain guiding you along
But you know it won't stay slow for long at all
When you soar down a hill and your screams echo out
But you will never know what will happen next
When you finish you will probably want to go on again
But your parents might not let you have another
Roller-coaster journey!

Connor Eddy (10)
Burnopfield Primary School

Fire

I love the heat of a red, glowing fire
When the flames dance and flicker like a candle in the wind
The flames spit into the night sky
Like a demented dragon woken from his sleep
I like fire
But then it starts to die away
Like a dragon resting
When the fire goes out
There are no flames dancing
No spitting flames
Just glowing embers
Like a tired, resting dragon.

Adam Piper (10)
Burnopfield Primary School

The Seaside

The seaside is where I like to go
And walk along its shingle shore.
We look inside rock pools
Where small crabs and fish are hiding.

In the summer we like to bathe
But we must watch out for the monstrous wave.
The lifeguard is always looking out
If we're in danger, he'll hear our shout.

At the end of the day, it's time to eat
Off to the shops for our favourite treat.
We like fish and chips and then ice cream
Today has been like a nice dream.

Lauren Clark (11)
Burnopfield Primary School

Donkeys

Clip-clop, clip-clop,
Down the road they trot,
Their swishy little tails
Are twitching fish.

Eeore, eeore,
Eyes like half moons
And great big ears,
Fluffy, grey coats and furry feet.

Yee hup, yee hup,
Tapping, moving on,
Taking loads and bags,
As the sun smiles down.

Num-num, num-num,
Feed time at last,
Munching like parrots on nuts and seeds,
Lights are out . . .
Night-night donkeys!

Jordan Crerar (11)
Burnopfield Primary School

Silence

I hate it!
When you have just been told off,
There is that awful
Silence.
The way you can hear,
Leaves flow outside,
Swish . . . swash . . . swish . . . swash.
The way you can hear,
Tennis ball to racket,
Bounce . . . hit . . . bounce . . . hit . . . hit.
The way you can hear,
Pen to paper in an exam,
Squiggle . . . squiggle . . . squiggle.

I hate it!

Silence is sweet
Silence is golden
Well . . .
To some people
But not
Me!
Silence is deafening.
I hate it!

Jayne Edwards (11)
Burnopfield Primary School

Blue

Blue is the colour of a bright summer sky.
Blue is the colour of my eyes,
Blue are my fingers on an icy cold day,
Blue is the colour of a huge blue whale.

The oceans and seas are a beautiful blue,
Bluebells in the park, there are more than a few,
Parrots in the rainforest, largest ever saw,
Are the dazzling, rich blue hyacinth macaws.

Of all the lovely colours in the world to see,
There's nothing better than blue, it's special to me.

Mark Eglintine (11)
Burnopfield Primary School

Dogs

I love *dogs!*
Loads of soft fur all around,
Even touching the dusty ground.
With their collars so bright,
You can even see them through the night.
Their paws so small,
They can even kick a ball.
Their teeth are so white,
They can even give you a scary bite.
Their whiskers are so tickly,
Like a green spiky bush so prickly.

Rachel Hewitson (10)
Burnopfield Primary School

The Jazzmanian Devil

My dog, Jazz, is a really daft dog,
She jumps up and down like the Crazy Frog.

She chases pigeons across the grass,
She really is a silly, young lass!

She steals my socks right off my feet
And then runs away into the street!

Every morning to wake me up,
She licks my face, the silly pup!

She eats everything if it doesn't move,
It doesn't even have to be food!

Even though she chewed my Newcastle hat,
I still think she is better than any old cat!

For a little dog, she's quite a rebel,
That's why we call her the Jazzmanian Devil.

Richard Albone (10)
Burnopfield Primary School

A Trip To The Zoo

Looking at the lions,
Looking at the snakes,
Looking at the crocodiles
That live in murky lakes.

Looking at the monkeys,
Looking at the hogs,
The ones that live in squidgy mud
And revolting bogs.

Looking at the tigers,
Looking at the bears,
Looking at the badgers,
Hiding in their lairs.

Looking at the gates,
To the end of the zoo,
I would like to go again,
I don't know about you!

Lauren Hoult (10)
Burnopfield Primary School

The Oak

The old oak stood proud and tall like a rocket
In the wintry back garden.
In the snow with its arms stretched out
And no leaves in sight.
Spring comes and the buds appear
Waiting to sprout into leaves.
By summer the leaves are green
And the birds are nesting high.
The tree is standing in the sun
Like someone on a beach.
Autumn comes, the winds blow
And leaves fall like rain.
Then it starts again.

Bruce Maddison (10)
Burnopfield Primary School

The Storm

Do you remember
When we were in the
Middle of the storm
Out at sea?

Do you remember
The waves hitting
The boat and making
Me sway side to side
Like a bus going across a
Rickety old bridge?

Do you remember
The boat
How everything on the boat
Went overboard?

Do you remember
How the waves nearly
Pushed the boat against some rocks?

Do you remember?

Iain Monkley (11)
Burnopfield Primary School

The Cheetah Was Here

This morning at dawn,
The cheetah came.
A gangster's silhouette,
A spark!
A flame!
Spots like coal,
A dark, menacing shadow,
Haunting us perfect deer.
That's when we'd say,
The cheetah was here!

The silent running,
The panting,
Like a fast running stream.
The smell of fresh meat lies in the savannah.
That's when we'd say,
The cheetah was here!

I hear the panting,
As the birds fly away.
A rustle of the grass,
With the gentle sway.
That's when I know,
The cheetah is here!

Rosie Bath (10)
Burnopfield Primary School

Spring

I like spring.
Pink and white blossom
On the bare trees,
Little lambs bouncing in the fields.
Flowers are blooming,
Like little fairies coming out to play.
The days are getting warmer
And the nights are getting lighter.
The summer is coming soon.
I like spring,
Do you?

Amie Blair (10)
Burnopfield Primary School

Do You Remember The Beach?

Do you remember the beach?
The sand that whispers, the shells that sing
And the waves crashing, *crash . . . crash.*

Do you remember the beach?
The morning sunshine swaying from side to side
And the seagulls squawking for their food.

Do you remember the beach?
The boats bobbing in the harbour,
Screaming for freedom.
Shells lying, decorating the seabed.

Do you remember the beach?
The waves rolling up the sand,
Sending crabs scurrying, hurrying . . .

Do you remember the beach?
The way we used to play years ago?

I remember the beach.

Abby Bailey (10)
Burnopfield Primary School

My Orange Day

I open my curtains and see the sunrise.
It is covering the sky like an orange rug,
I know it must be Orange Wednesday!

For lunch I have carrot soup
And an orange cup filled with orange juice.
For dessert I have a piece of carrot cake.

I get in the car to go to swimming,
Guess which colour car I see?
Blue!
I get to swimming and everyone's face is orange.
Oh yes, I have orange-tinted goggles.

I go to bed
And I see the sunset,
It looks like a dragon's fiery breath.

David Alexander (10)
Burnopfield Primary School

The Seasons

Winter is here
And the ground is covered with a thick blanket of snow.
Robins fill the air with sweet songs,
As snow falls softly to the ground.
Icicles hang, like sharp knives that fall and smash like glass.

Spring is here
And lambs bounce about, like fluffy clouds.
Trees wake up from a deep sleep
And brand new buds burst out,
Like baby birds hatching from their eggs.
Hedgehogs stretch
As they leave their long winter sleep behind.

Summer is here.
The sun comes out to say hello and warm the earth.
Flowers bloom,
Filling the gardens with rainbows of colour
And the air is perfumed with sweet-smelling scents.
On light nights you can hear happy children
Playing in the streets.

Autumn is here
And leaves turn into bright colours of gold, red and brown,
That look like a carpet of fiery flames.
Branches are bare and crooked,
Like a witch's fingers.
Bonfires burn brightly
And fill the air with eerie smoke.

Victoria Allinson (10)
Burnopfield Primary School

Fire

Crackling red blanket of heat,
Warming the musty midnight,
Polluting the atmosphere.

Dancing wildly, it spreads
And more spirits join in the dance
And party till morn.

When its enemy, rain, patters down,
It battles courageously
To keep its head high.
But finally, rain gets tough
And all that is left is black death,
To sizzle on the cold, damp grass.

But fire will come back tomorrow night.
Fire.

Nick McCarton (10)
Burnopfield Primary School

Autumn

I adore autumn
When the leaves fall off trees
Like flying toffee wrappers.

I adore it
When the sycamore seeds fall like twisting spirals
And look fabulous.

I adore it
When the leaves blow round like a mini tornado
Ready to wipe out a city.

Ben Railton (10)
Burnopfield Primary School

Pink

Pink is bright, cool and funky.
It's like a million stars in a moonlit sky.
It's top of the colour chart.
It's like funky *hip hop* music.
Have you seen it?
Pink is like a star that never stops shining.
Have you seen it?

Rebecca Stoddart (10)
Burnopfield Primary School

Day 1 To Goodbye

My first day is but a haze
In shiny shoes I walk round the maze
My mammy's gone, I'm left alone
A room full of strangers
I want to go home

Bumps and scrapes along the way
Learning new things every day
Meeting new teachers and classrooms too
A nightmare when Mr Wood was fixing the loo

My pencil case torn
My shoes are now scuffed
But I've made lots of new friends
We've had laughs
We've had huffs

It's all gone so fast
We're now in Year 6
We're now to be shuffled
We'll have to re-mix

Goodbye to friends and teachers too
We're off to schools where everything's new
With all the tears and good wishes said
Burnopfield will always be in my head

From Mrs Hunter to Mrs Hopper
Mr Lenaghan too
And those in-between
I'd just like to thank all of you.

Hollie Stokes (10)
Burnopfield Primary School

Cat

My cat, Figo, goes mad every night,
He runs backwards and forwards,
From the window to the door,
As fast as lightning, so he cannot stop,
He skids on the floor and bumps into the door.

My cat, Figo, gets tired every night,
He curls up on the mat in front of the fire,
Like a giant cotton wool ball,
He lies as still as a rock,
But as quiet as a mouse,
Until it is time for me to go to bed
And he comes up too.

James Taylor (10)
Burnopfield Primary School

Blue!

I love the colour blue because
It is the colour of the sea,
Where everybody swims until
Half-past three.
I love the colour blue because
It's the colour of the sky,
Where clouds pass by.
I love the colour blue.

Marc Clews (11)
Burnopfield Primary School

My Best Friend

This is my best friend.
My best friend is hairy,
He's crazy and silly.
He runs into doors,
He runs into chairs,
He'll sleep in a basket,
He'll run up the stairs.
This is my best friend.
My best friend he smiles,
He's funny and very stupid.
He won't play football,
He won't play tennis,
He'll lie on his back,
He'll jump at you.
My best friend is my dog!

Lewis Shipley (11)
Burnopfield Primary School

Paint!

Splat! Squelch!
Paint on the paper,
This way,
That way,
Up and down,
Painting a pretty picture!
Big brushes,
Little brushes,
All different-sized brushes.
Painting on the paper
Like seagulls swooping in the sea.
Head up high,
Splashing paint on the paper.

Kirsty Bell (10)
Burnopfield Primary School

Wolves

They live in the woods,
They hunt like a falcon,
Howl!
Their coats are covered in snow-like fur,
Their eyes gleam in the dark forest,
King of the dog species,
They hunt with their fangs
Which are like daggers
And they howl in the moon's light.
Howl! Howl!

Andrew Booth (10)
Burnopfield Primary School

Beyond The Shadows

The wind whistles through the branches
In the darkness of the night.
The glittering moon casts shadows
Over the dark streets and houses.

The town is deserted, winter is coming
And no one will dare walk the streets.
Frost covers the windows
And the streets are covered in cold ice.
The air is as sharp as a dagger.

The street lights flicker,
Nothing can brighten this deserted town.
Winter is coming,
Who will dare walk the streets?

Richard Urwin (10)
Burnopfield Primary School

Blue

Blue, blue, have you seen a colour as blue?
Light and dark, how it dazzles you.
It lights up the sky and darkens the sky.
It is the colour of my friend's eyes.
Blue is the colour of the sea, even the rain is blue.
Oh! how it dazzles you.
It's blue, blue, blue.
Do you remember blue? Do you?

Ryan Mitchell-Hird (10)
Burnopfield Primary School

Elephants

I like elephants,
They are like a marching band
When they are walking by on land.
When they run,
They have so much fun.
They lounge around in the sun,
Just because they weigh a ton.
They are so fat,
Because of that.
They don't like mice,
Because they're not very nice.
Their trunks are thin, very long
And when they sneeze, it sounds like a gong.
I'd like to go on holiday and see them in the wild,
Because I have only seen them in zoos as a child.

Emily Robinson (10)
Burnopfield Primary School

A Winter Poem

The world is white and wonderful now the winter's here,
The trees are dressed in their Sunday best, shimmering, frosty, cold.
Little robin with his bright red breast sings high up above,
To tell the world that winter's here, the season that we love.

Cameron Holliday (10)
Burnopfield Primary School

Seasonal Colours

Green is the colour we meet every day,
January, February, March, April, May.
Green is the colour of gardens that grow,
I always like to watch the flower show.

Yellow is the colour that I love to remember,
Through June, July, August and September.
Sun shining brightly for most of the day,
Children outside as they laugh and play.

Red is the colour of warm embers,
That I feel through October, November and December.
Trudging through the woods collecting berries,
Wrapped up warm with hat, scarf and wellies.

Laura Callaghan (10)
Burnopfield Primary School

I Love The Seasons

I love the seasons,
When the leaves start to grow,
The colour is unleashed,
All because of spring.
I love the seasons,
When all the kids are running
Up and down the street,
Like shooting stars flying through the sky,
All because of summer.
I love the seasons,
When the leaves put on their golden robes
And when they flicker through the air,
Like pixies dancing at a ball,
All because of autumn.
I love the seasons,
When the snowflakes fall from side to side,
With their glittery coats wrapped around them
And snowballs flying through the air like bombs in war,
All because of winter.
I love the seasons.

Luke Nuttall (10)
Burnopfield Primary School

The Last Dragon

Under a rocky hillside,
In a dirty, mossy cave,
Lay the crusty old dragon,
Whose life must be saved.

As cold as the grave
And the stone brick wall,
As cold as the gold spilt for his bed,
The last ever dragon's life,
Is near to an end.

His heartbeat drops rapidly,
Like a boulder off a cliff,
Life seems to pass,
Into an endless drift.

Breathing gets shallow,
As life seems to part,
A hundred more lifetimes,
Pass away today.

The moon comes out,
To wave goodbye,
As the life of the dragon,
Begins to die.

I hear one last gasp,
Where there once was a roar,
The very last dragon,
Is breathing no more.

The dragons have gone,
After hundreds of years,
There won't be anymore,
No one you can trace,
As for the last dragon,
He can't be replaced.

Lucy Horsman (11)
Burnopfield Primary School

Chocolate

I adore chocolate, do you?
It's so delightful
I wish I could eat it day and night
Chocolate moon, chocolate stars
The universe is a chocolate bar

It's like snakes when melted on cakes
I adore chocolate, do you?
It's giant toffee monsters chasing me
If only everything was chocolate!
Chocolate cats, chocolate dogs
Even chocolate mums and dads
Yum-yum
I adore chocolate, do you?
I know I do.

Kurtis Pearson (9)
Burnopfield Primary School

I Love Winter!

I love winter,
Plunging into a white blanket of snow,
Then throwing ice-cold snowballs at each other,
Making a snowman,
Then putting a scarf, hat and carrot on its body,
Snowflakes falling on our noses,
Icicles hanging from the tree branches,
Making angel shapes in the snow,
Snowflakes dancing in the sky
Like fairies greeting each other,
Then having hot, steamy soup beside the fire,
That's why I love winter!

Sophie Parker (10)
Burnopfield Primary School

The Seasons

Springtime is upon us,
Warmer, brighter days,
Flowers budding, birds singing,
A time for new beginnings.

Summer sun high in the sky,
Holidays to take and running wild,
Down to the beach, the sea nice and calm,
Seagulls swooping down to the shore.

Autumn arrives, leaves are swirling,
Colours are blazing red, orange and brown,
The wind whistles through the trees,
Winter is fast approaching.

Winter brings snow and ice,
Christmas is coming, presents to open,
Snowflakes falling all around us,
Everywhere still, quiet and hushed.

Rebecca Armstrong (11)
Burnopfield Primary School

Fire

A poem about fire,
Is the world's desire.
When the fire burns,
It's like a rocket
Flying out of the atmosphere.
Fire is the Devil's best friend,
It crackles, it creaks and it burns!

A poem about fire,
Is the heart of evil.
When they glare at you with those bright, red eyes,
They stab things with their flaming weapons.
Those poor, unfortunate souls,
Are ruined by evil fire!

A poem about fire,
Is horrible to hear.
When they crackle and they creak, it's disgusting,
Sometimes it can be good, but mostly bad.
Even flames so small,
Can cause big, big chaos.

Conor Reeve (11)
Burnopfield Primary School

Fairies

Fairies in pink,
Fairies in blue,
Fairies that look after you.

Fairies in yellow,
Fairies in green,
The prettiest fairies you've ever seen.

Fairies in skirts,
Fairies in dresses,
Oh my goodness, so many guesses.

Fairies that sparkle,
Fairies that glow,
Fairies that can create a rainbow.

Whatever fairies I'll meet tonight,
I think it's time to snuggle up tight
And dream . . . dream of . . . fairies.

Rachael Edmunds (10)
Burnopfield Primary School

Trampolining

Do you remember?
We were at Athens, just you and me.
Standing on the floor, waiting, waiting.
Do you remember?
Getting on, just you, then me.
Soaring, whizzing, bouncing up and down.
Do you remember?
Somersaulting, twisting, just you and me,
Just like a bird in the sky.
Do you remember?
Seeing our marks, just you and me.
They were brilliant, fantastic, superb.
Do you remember?
Standing on the podium, you beside me,
Me with gold, you with silver.
Do you remember?
Emotions flying high, just you and me,
So happy, inexplicable feelings.
We were there,
At the Olympics.
Do you remember?
Athens.

Maya Rockett (10)
Burnopfield Primary School

I Love Wind

I like wind,
Whoosh, whoosh, whoop, whoop,
The wind is here,
As it blows through the trees
And they're talking to me,
The wind is here,
Blowing round trees,
Scattering leaves,
Making the air go cold,
See flags flying,
See kites soaring,
Dancing in the midday sun,
The wind is here,
Its children laughing,
Whooping, wailing,
A perfect warning noise,
I like wind,
Blowing breezes, roaring rain,
Lion-like lightning, stalking the stormy sky,
I like wind,
The wind is here, the wind is here,
Suddenly clearing, I see sun,
I hate sun!
But I love wind.

Sophie Fraser (11)
Burnopfield Primary School

School

Teachers can be good
Teachers can be bad
Mostly bossy
Stack them books up
Pack your bag
They always tell you
In command
Children can be good
Children can be bad
Mostly well-behaved
Yes Sir
No Sir
We are never in command.

Luke Nevin (10)
Burnopfield Primary School

Enjoying The Park

The park is an enjoyable place to play,
So feed the swans right away.
Listen to the birds high and low,
The park is a wonderful place to go.
Have an ice cream and enjoy the day,
Watch the children have a play.
Hear the crunching of the leaves,
The beautiful scent of the flowers,
Look all around and see the towers.

Monira Miah (9)
Hadrian Primary School

The Monster

Where does it hide?
Is it under my bed,
Or am I insane and it's inside my head?
It's taller than a house,
Sneakier than a mouse,
With dark, black eyes of evil,
His nose like a pointy knife,
A mouth with just a tongue sticking out,
No lips,
The scary monster's body is like a porcupine,
With spikes on his back and on his tummy.
What you would call feet are bigger than me now,
With nails like cardboard boxes, don't ask me how,
His voice is like shrieking cats, all with a different pitch,
Now he's become my best friend, I call him Mitch!

Laura Craig (10)
Hadrian Primary School

Alien!

I heard about him in books
I heard about him from people
I saw pictures of his ugly looks
The alien is invading!

I saw the spaceship circle
It landed on the ground
Then the graceful, charming door
Opened at my feet around.

Then a slimy green thing
That smelt rather sick
Came out of the door
With a little wooden stick.

He came up to me
It was quite a scare
And then in a little voice
This is what he said,

'Don't be scared of me
Even though I'm rather rare
I have come from planet Mars
And I'm not very fond of cars.'

I thought to myself, *let's be friends*
As I have never seen him before,
'I've come to give you this to send
To my best friend now.'

Jennifer Boyack (9)
Hadrian Primary School

The Winter Wind

The trees were blowing in the blue, winter sky
The sun was trying to warm us up.

The winter wind was blowing on us
Freezing my nose, my ears and my toes!

Bethanni Petersen (8)
Hadrian Primary School

The Sea

I am swimming in the sea to see what I can see,
I can see fish trying to tickle my feet with their small tails,
I can see a boat pulling in, bobbing up and down,
Like a gymnast on a trampoline.

Now I've swum in the sea,
I can see the beach and see the people lying on mats
Burning like an oven,
What a lovely day,
But sadly I must go away!

Jacob Jackson (9)
Hadrian Primary School

The Sea

Look at the reflected, blue, salty sea
With graceful fish swimming joyfully

Look at the sea grabbing the sand
With children playing happily
And getting it on their hands

Look at the ferry bobbing along the sea
With millions of people
Enjoying their hot, lovely tea!

Thameenah Akhtar (9)
Hadrian Primary School

The River

Gentle dancing ripples floating across the river,
When the journey starts, it almost ends,
Fierce crashing waves hurling swiftly at the immense, creaky bridge
And seagulls soaring through the sky like flying saucers.

Even though we don't have a train or car,
We still have a metal kayak
And a two-people carrier ferry
And we need some information books.

As well as a million pounds in a cheque,
So we can buy a car and a train
And we will be able to finish our journey across the river,
So now we will find our kayak and journey across the sea.

With ripples so beautiful, we can see them shimmer,
When we end our journey across the sea.

Joshua Anderson (8)
Hadrian Primary School

The Emperor's Garden

In the emperor's garden, blossom floats gently
Above the flavoured plants
The holy bonsais dancing in a gust of a swift wind
As they dance gracefully, their roots on a slant.

Butterflies flutter, carrying Heaven on their wings
Sweet buzzing of the bees
As they bob their tiny bodies through the flowers
And that blessed song that the blue tits sing.

As he approaches his golden palace of light
He looks back and sees these wonders
That glow during the moonlit night.

Adam Ramsey (9)
Hadrian Primary School

In The River

Aqua smooth waters ripple with fear
When the jaws of the red tuna come too near,
The glum little shrimps darts this way and that!
Malicious old rubbish, old rubbish
Crushing colossal environments,
Gratified prawns not in the nets,
Now they can go collect the money from their bets.

Fishes in poverty and fishes in love,
They all have to look out for what is above,
The water will freeze, then melt,
Then a redecorations is in with burnt umber
And yellow ochre
And . . .
Oh dear, what a hit below the belt!

Maisie McCormack (10)
Hadrian Primary School

Spring

The winter is gone, so the animals come out to play,
From the hibernation, to the new creation,
The winter has gone and a new world begun,

The newborn lambs are here to see the new world,
Little foals learning how to run gracefully,
The delightful ducklings wanting to swim, just like their mum.

The daffodils springing,
While the new world's beginning,
It's the best time to see!

Rachael Lindsay (9)
Hadrian Primary School

The Beach

The golden sand shining in the sun,
Crabs darting from side to side,
Children splashing in the massive salty ocean.
Sand flying everywhere from dogs digging furiously,
Boats trying to catch fish,
Ships sailing on a cruise,
Music blasting from the fair.
These are my favourite things about the beach.

Curtis Stephenson (10)
Hadrian Primary School

School

Ding-a-ling-a-ling goes the bell for school
All the chattery children hear it and drool
Teacher's stressed, though it has only been ten minutes
Her class has already pushed her over the limits

So they set off working, trying not to giggle
Sitting still but starting to squiggle
Scribble, scribble, goes the pen on the paper
The talking gets louder five minutes later

Tick, tick-tock goes the clock on the wall
Just fifteen minutes and they'll be rushing, rushing down the hall
Running because it is half-past three
Going as fast as they can, because they want their tea.

Jade Doran (10)
Hadrian Primary School

Summer

The sunshine is hot and scalding in the summer's sky within
The birds must be boiling when they pass the burning sun
The sea is hot in summer, that's why people go and swim
Seagulls paddling forcefully to get to the water's edge.

Beaches must be packed with children having fun
Crabs sinking into the sand, making sure they don't get noticed
So they can nip children's toes
The fairground is open now because it is lovely and hot
Children going on the ghost train to get a frightening shock.

Summer is drifting away now, the sea is getting cold
Minchella's ice creams are no good now
Because they won't cool you down
The fairground tickets are all gone now, so you can't have some fun
The roller coaster has broken down now
Because too many people have been on it
Next year summer will be back to have some fun at the fair.

Grace Anne Davison (9)
Hadrian Primary School

The River

The river is a lovely place
But do you know what lurks underneath?
Fish live in the river
But they are scaly and slimy.
You might like frogs
But their jump makes you quiver and shiver.
Frogs jump so gracefully
But the sea is not their cup of tea.
So fish that swim and frogs that jump
Live in the river so happily.

Robyn Kelly (8)
Hadrian Primary School

The Beach

Children playing on the beach as their mums look on
Immense waves crashing on the huge rocks
The disgusting waste on the pier
The sand lying as flat as paper
Heads popping out of the water
Balls bouncing about.

Ryan Just (9)
Hadrian Primary School

Summer's Day

People playing in the park on this summer's day
Birds swooping through the air on this summer's day
When children of Year 4 and 5 come and spoil their day
Gracefully grow the flowers
The boys in the park doing their skateboard tricks
And now the sun has gone down
So we say goodbye.

Courtney Price (9)
Hadrian Primary School

Rainforest

An aqua of whistling and howling fills the baby forest,
Tropical, multicoloured birds swoop and swish, singing indescribable tunes,
Huge, twisted ponga trees reach up high into the pure, sweet-scented sky,
Monkeys and gorillas fight over bananas in the wild,
Waterfalls crash off dry ground and transform into quick-flowing rivers,
Feathered herons plunge their arrow-like heads into Pluto-cold water to find silver, scaly fish,
But then, when the thunder starts to crackle and heavens start to flow,
That's when the beasts of the forests decide, to go . . .

Carl Stimpson (9)
Hadrian Primary School

If I Were . . .

If I were an astronaut,
I'd go up into space!
If I were a clown,
I'd pull a funny face!

If I were a teacher,
I'd stand up straight and tall.
If I were a footballer,
I'd always have the ball.

If I were a TV presenter,
I'd read out all the news.
If I were an electrician,
I'd fix a broken fuse.

If I were a writer,
I'd write a fairy tale.
If I were a diver,
I'd swim with an enormous whale!

But I'm none of these, I'm me,
And that's who I want to be!

Olivia Close (11)
Newbottle Primary School

Excitement . . .

Excitement is the taste of mango.
Excitement is the colour of sand.
Excitement is the smell of pineapple.
Excitement is the sound of the crashing waves.
Excitement looks like the Caribbean islands.
Excitement is going to Jamaica.

Lewis Hemmings (10)
Newbottle Primary School

Sports!

Playing tennis, it's the second set,
I hit the ball over the net.
Playing golf in the burning sun,
Hooray! It's a hole in one!
Playing rugby, the ball in my hands,
Everyone watching me from the stands.
Playing football, you won't regret,
When you get the ball in the back of the net.

Sam Thompson (11)
Newbottle Primary School

Our School

Our school is the coolest,
The best I've ever known,
The teachers are the funniest,
They make me laugh and groan.

The children are the brightest
And are definitely no fools,
English and maths are boring,
But PE is so cool.

Oh no! The weekend's coming fast,
For most of us anyway,
Apart from the girl who locked herself
In the cupboard only yesterday.

Charlotte Merritt (11)
Newbottle Primary School

Little Old Joe

There once was a boy called Little Old Joe,
Who found he had no big toe.
He laughed and cried,
And always tried to hide.
His mother ran with a frying pan
And shouted, 'Come and play!
Now come and you will shout hooray!'
Little Old Joe tripped over his lace
And now he's in a running race.
He found his toe and stuck it on with glue,
But now he can't take off his shoe!

Danielle Mustard (11)
Newbottle Primary School

Gold

My happy colour is shiny, sparkly gold.
The taste is like sweet birthday cake.
It looks like a lovely bunny.
It sounds like a peaceful waterfall.
It feels like a rabbit's soft fur.
It smells like my mam's lasagne.
Gold makes me feel cheerful inside.

Daniel Dixon (11)
Newbottle Primary School

Not What I Wanted

Hey, Mr Santa Claus,
Where's my shiny bike?
There's a load of junk here
And nothing that I like.
I've read your letter
And I've come to see you twice,
Don't you give me a ho, ho, ho,
You forgot my shiny bike.

Hey, Mr Santa Claus,
Where's my baby pram?
You promised me you'd get me one,
You remember who I am?
I'm that little girl who sat right upon your knee,
Don't you give me a ho, ho, ho,
You forgot my baby pram.

Declan Garrigan (10)
Newbottle Primary School

Getting Out Of Bed

Getting out of bed,
Oh, what an awful chore,
First you have to open your eyes
And try to find the floor.
Stumbling down the stairs,
Trying not to fall,
But with my eyes practically shut,
I bash into the wall.
What a strange, unearthly feeling,
But it's school's fault with what I'm dealing!

Jessica Taylor (11)
Newbottle Primary School

Unicorn Head

Last night my brother was annoying me,
When all of a sudden a wizard appeared,
He said a spell, '1, 2, 3,'
The night my brother was annoying me.

'Unicorn white, unicorn red,
Unicorn black, unicorn head.'

Sparks then flew from his wand,
And after that my brother was stunned.
He clicked his fingers three more times,
Then said the spell again, a rhyme.

My brother's head wasn't normal any more,
It was a unicorn's head peeping around the door.

Stephanie Short (10)
Newbottle Primary School

My Hero

My hero is special
I see him every day
I really do love him
In every single way
He helps me with my homework
He even makes my tea
He loves his football, just like me
It's my dad, don't you see?

Elliot Salicki (11)
Newbottle Primary School

On My Way To School

I don't like going to school
The route is very strange
I would take the bus
But I haven't any change.
I have to pass a man called Stan
He's a bit loony in the head
And then there's this weird kid
Who's scared of a four-poster bed.
I have to go through this dark wood
Where I always end up tripping in mud
And then I go through an ugly pea-green gate
After that I'm in a horrible state.
I finally reach the school with a giant mud stain
It's worse coming home because I have to go through it all again.

Katie Walvin (11)
Newbottle Primary School

My Pink And Purple Zebra

The problem is my pink and purple zebra's gone astray,
Never ever will it come back again.
I remember holding the reins,
Galloping down the little road,
My zebra went in slow mode.
Now that's when I fell off down the road,
Then my zebra went in fast mode.
But anyway, we sold the stupid thing,
Now I've got a pony
And it's called Balony!

Brittany Hayes (10)
Newbottle Primary School

Diamond Is The Best Dog Ever!

Diamond is the best dog ever,
She is very, very clever.
She is white, black and brown
And is funny like a clown.
She has a lovely sister and brother
And we really, really love her.
She has a lovely family and home,
I hope she likes this poem.

Katie Howe (10)
Newbottle Primary School

A View From A Hotel Window

I look out my hotel window,
Onto a beautiful, glistening beach.
Surfers swallowed by the mighty blue waves,
Children's sandcastles destroyed by the incoming tide,
Their parents sunbathing on their colourful towels,
The view from my hotel window.

Gary Embleton (10)
Newbottle Primary School

Happiness

Happiness is pink,
Happiness tastes like a hot chocolate drink,
Happiness smells like candyfloss,
Happiness is like a holiday is sunny Cos,
Happiness sounds like birds tweeting in a tree,
Happiness feels like my dog licking me.

Robyn Owens (10)
Newbottle Primary School

Ten Naughty Children

(Based on 'Ten Naughty Schoolboys' by AA Milne)

Ten naughty children being good and fine,
One child fainted, then there were nine.

Nine naughty children eating their bait,
One got knocked out by a sandwich, then there were eight.

Eight naughty children want to go to Heaven,
One went to Hell, then there were seven.

Seven naughty children playing with sticks,
One hit a boy and then there were six.

Six naughty children glad to be alive,
One got shot, then there were five.

Five naughty children really want to grow,
One shrank too much, then there were four.

Four naughty children doing RE,
One fell off his chair, then there were three.

Three naughty children, one had the flu,
He went to hospital, then there were two.

Two naughty children want to go home,
One called his mam, then there was one.

One naughty child playing on his own,
He got really bored and ran all the way home,
Then there were none.

Rebecca Wilson (11)
Newbottle Primary School

Who Am I?

Who am I?
Am I a boy or girl?
What am I like?
Brave? Shy?
I stare at the pearl
Trying to remember
What's burning inside me?
An ember?
What's my name?
Kelly? Lee?
Suddenly, it flashes back to me!
I know my name!
Whack, whack, whack!
It was . . . not again
People banging at the door
I know my name!
I'm falling to the floor
But now I've forgotten again!

Jessica Boal (11)
Newbottle Primary School

Sadness

I feel sad when I'm in the playground
As my heart is buried underground.
I'm thinking in my head
Where is the life I live?
From friends to family
The sound of people
The blurred figures in the air
I watch the clouds as they look and stare.
It's quite good because I'm luckier than some
Remember though, my heart is underground.

Carly Quigley (10)
Newbottle Primary School

If I Had Wings

(Based on 'If I Had Wings' by Pie Corbett)

If I had wings I would taste the cold air,
If I had wings I would smell the beautiful flowers,
If I had wings I would touch the highest tower,
If I had wings I would hear the aeroplanes going past,
If I had wings I would dream of reaching the bright stars.

Natalie Bell (10)
Newbottle Primary School

Sport

Sport is exciting, sport is cool
Just like football, golf or pool
Football rocks, football rules
Football is like expensive jewels
Bowls is concentration, you have to stay still
I'm waiting for something, I'm waiting for drill
But now I've got something to say,
'I'm sorry, but that is it for today.'

James Davison (11)
Newbottle Primary School

Sunderland FC

Studs are in the mud again,
Arca scores a goal,
Davis lets a whopper in,
Oh no, it's 7-2.
The crowd are going wild,
The team are losing hope,
Oh no!
The full-time whistle goes,
Sunderland freeze,
Liverpool cheer,
Sunderland lose again.

John Gatenby (10)
Newbottle Primary School

My Dog, Taz

My dog, Taz, is so great
She always jumps the garden gate
Taz has bright blue eyes
She always sits in the kitchen and cries
Taz does not pull on the lead
She would not bite and make you bleed
She is as friendly as can be
And always likes to have some tea
My dog, Taz, likes to sleep
And likes to make other dogs weep
My dog, Taz, is so clever
I'll love her forever and ever.

Rebecca Coyles (11)
Newbottle Primary School

A Dog

I had a dog
Cute he was
Ran around the house
Like a mad dog
He was fluffy
He was sweet
Chewed the seat belts on the car seat.

He was sad when we went away
He would be happy nearly every day
He jumped up high in the air
He splashed and shook water everywhere
Now he's gone
No friends to care
But he never left me
All I know, he's with me everywhere.

Catherine Moor (11)
Newbottle Primary School

What Is Red?

Red is blood dripping from my elbow
Red is an apple dripping from my mouth
Red is a fire engine up and down the streets
Red is noisy and loving.

Tiegan Crozier (7)
Newbottle Primary School

Touch!

Touch!
What can you feel?
The long, velvet neck
Of a baby giraffe,
The soft, fluffy fur
Of a Siamese cat.

Touch!
What can you feel?
The brown warty skin
Of a croaking, jumping toad,
The curly, poisonous tail
Of a stinging, dangerous scorpion.

Touch!
What can you feel?
The wet red tongue
Of a white dog licking me,
The rough brown bark
On the big, old oak tree.

Lucy McCabe (8)
Newbottle Primary School

What Is Red?

Red is juicy tomatoes,
Red is big, fat, juicy tomatoes,
Red is blood dripping from my mouth,
Red is lava in a volcano bubbling,
Red is apples crunching,
Red is a robin redbreast blowing in the wind,
Red is a tongue,
Red is a ladybird on a leaf,
Red is paint,
Red is excellent.

Scott Galley (8)
Newbottle Primary School

What Is Red?

Red is tomatoes, lovely as can be
Because the juice drips in my tea.
Red is strawberries, sweet and lovely,
Red is roses sweet and pretty.
Red is your heart pumping your blood,
Red is the sun setting.
Red is a water bottle that you drink from,
Red is a colour of the rainbow.
Red is a robin redbreast,
It goes cheep, cheep.
Red is a fire alarm call point,
Red is a bus that zooms fast.

Amy Riley (7)
Newbottle Primary School

Touch!

Touch!
What can you feel?
The soft yellow feathers
Of a cute, chirping chick.

Touch!
What can you feel?
The rubbery, damp skin
Of a plump, bouncy toad.
The sharp, venomous tail
Of a big, dangerous scorpion.

Touch!
What can you feel?
The long, brown, spotty neck
Of a tall, happy giraffe.
The curly, small tail
Of a sly, sneaky cat.

Rachael Brown (8)
Newbottle Primary School

What Is Red?

Red is blood dripping down my leg
Red is strawberries dripping down my cheeks
Red is the sun shining
Red is tomatoes, round and fat.

Patrick Coils (7)
Newbottle Primary School

Touch!

Touch!
What can you feel?
The dry, soft fur
Of a large cute panda bear.
The soft golden fluff
Of a tiny chick.

Touch!
What can you feel?
The wet, rubbery skin
Of a large green toad.
The sharp, deadly tail
Of a short, dangerous scorpion.

Touch!
What can you feel?
The wrinkly skin
Of an enormous grey elephant.
The soft white fur
Of a little white rabbit.

Anna Dean (8)
Newbottle Primary School

What Is Red?

Red is strawberries, beautiful and juicy.
Red is blood dripping from my finger.
Red is an apple, tender and lovely.
Red is a heart pumping blood around my body.

Chelsea Forster (7)
Newbottle Primary School

What Is Green?

Green is tasty grapes dripping down my top,
Green is the colour of my grass,
Green is my caterpillar eating a green leaf,
Green is a juicy pear dripping down my chin,
Green is a colour of the rainbow,
Green is my imagination skipping in the spring,
Green is the island.

Alisha Garrigan (8)
Newbottle Primary School

Touch!

Touch!
What can you feel?
The yellow fluffy fur
Of a tiny chick,
And a smooth petal
Curved over my hand.

Touch!
What can you feel?
The slimy, wet skin
Of a croaky, damp toad,
The sharp, poisonous,
Dangerous scorpion.

Touch!
What can you feel?
The monstrous, sharp teeth
Of a scary blue shark,
The friendly sharp spikes
Of a small brown hedgehog.

Hannah Goodman (7)
Newbottle Primary School

Touch!

Touch!
What can you feel?
The lovely white fur
Of a polar bear
The big fierce teeth
Of a blue shark

Touch!
What can you feel?
The bumpy, green skin
Of a big green toad
The big dark tail
Of a big black scorpion.

Michael Jones (7)
Newbottle Primary School

What Is Yellow?

Yellow is butter dripping from my toast,
Yellow is a juicy lemon,
Yellow is the sun shining in my eyes,
Yellow is bananas, juicy and nice,
Yellow is a person's hair,
Yellow is a crayon,
Yellow is happy,
Yellow is sweet, nice and juicy.

Laurie Naisbitt (7)
Newbottle Primary School

What Is Blue?

Blue is rain trickling down the drain.
Blue is blueberries, sweet and juicy.
Blue is the sky outside.
Blue is my water bottle.
Blue is water dripping from the sky.
Blue is my pen at school.
Blue is my school jumper.
Blue is happiness.

Jasmine Pearson (7)
Newbottle Primary School

What Is Red?

Red is a fire engine, *splash, splash, splash.*
Red is an apple swinging on a tree.
Red is lava bubbling in a volcano.
Red is a robin's breast waving in the wind.
Red is a ladybird sitting on the fence.
Red makes me happy.

Kalem Robson (7)
Newbottle Primary School

Touch!

Touch!
What can you feel?
The long, spotty, smooth, patterned, yellow giraffe.
The little, cute, warm and furry baby chick.

Touch!
What can you feel?
The massive, heavy body of an enormous, fat elephant.
The furry, warm body of a tiny ginger cat.

Touch!
What can you feel?
The damp, rubbery skin of a jumping, croaking toad.
The stinging, sharp tail of a tiny, dangerous scorpion.

Laura Shaw (7)
Newbottle Primary School

What Is Red?

Red is strawberry juice dripping from my chin.
Red is tomatoes, all juicy and round.
Red is a big certificate that you win.
Red is blood dripping from my skin.
Red is a big heart that pumps blood around my body.
Red is a big, red pen to write with.
Red is the sun setting in the sky.
Red is my mobile.
Red is a Babybel cheese that I eat.
Red is a water bottle that I drink from.

Katie Smith (7)
Newbottle Primary School

What Is Brown?

Brown is sweet, sugary chocolate.
Brown is shiny hair shimmering in the sun.
Brown is horrible hair dye, it gets all over your hands.
Brown is poor people who live on the streets.
Brown is thick, squashy mud.
Brown is cake that smells like chocolate.

Bethany Straughan (8)
Newbottle Primary School

Touch

Touch!
What can you feel?
A sharp fin of a scary shark,
The smooth, wet skin of a friendly dolphin.

Touch!
What can you feel?
The rubbery, damp skin of a croaky-voiced toad,
The dangerous, strong tail of a mad and unkind scorpion.

Jessica Thompson (7)
Newbottle Primary School

Touch!

Touch!
What can you feel?
The friendly, purring fur
Of a blackish, brownish cat,
The long, spotty neck
Of a tall, thin giraffe.

Touch!
What can you feel?
The sharp, vicious tail
Of a deadly, poisonous scorpion,
The soft, warm, cute body
Of a yellow chirping chick.

Lauren Vosper (7)
Newbottle Primary School

Touch!

Touch!
What can you feel?
The sharp, dry spikes
Of a spiky, rough hedgehog.

Touch!
What can you feel?
The sharp, pointy teeth
Of a large grey shark.

Touch!
What can you feel?
The sharp, poisonous tail
Of a tiny, dangerous scorpion.

Ellis Williamson (7)
Newbottle Primary School

Touch!

Touch!
What can you feel?
The smooth grey skin
Of a swimming shark,
A little, brown, furry bear
Smiling at me.

Touch!
What can you feel?
The dry, rubbery skin
Of a large green toad,
The sharp, poisonous tail
Of a small, dangerous scorpion.

Christopher James Tilley (7)
Newbottle Primary School

Touch!

Touch!
What can you feel?
The rough pavement
In the old yard.

Touch!
What can you feel?
The rubbery, damp skin
Of a jumping slimy toad.

Jake Wilson (8)
Newbottle Primary School

What Is Yellow?

Yellow is the sand in my feet,
Yellow is my hair, long and soft,
Yellow is bananas on a tree,
Yellow is daffodils blowing in the wind,
Yellow is beautiful and bright,
Yellow is friendly,
Yellow is kind,
Yellow is happy,
Yellow is fireworks,
Yellow is a colour.

Chloe Britton (7)
Newbottle Primary School

What Is Red?

Red is a heart beating up and down
Red is strawberries, sweet and juicy
Red is apples, lovely and lush
Red is juicy tomatoes dripping down my shirt
Red is nail polish, gorgeous and red
Red is a sunset up in the sky
Red is a mango, good to smell
Gorgeous red berries, juicy and tasty
Red is lipstick, rosy and red
Red is jam, great and lush.

Emma Callender (7)
Newbottle Primary School

My Little Baby Sister

My little baby sister, only three days old,
She wriggles and jiggles when she's in my arms,
I'm starting to feel a bit sick now,
Oh no, get her off!
Right, she's done it this time,
She's been sick all over my top!

Alexandra Hepple (9)
Newbottle Primary School

Happiness

Happiness is when you wake up to find it's Sunday.
Happiness is when it's snowing outside.
Happiness is when I get a new game.
Happiness is when you see a horror film.
Happiness is when you get a new Star Wars DVD.
Happiness is when you get a new pack of Pokémon cards.
Happiness is when I play football with my friends.
Happiness is when you're off school.
Happiness is when you go swimming.
Happiness is a way of life.

Jamie Oliver (8)
Newbottle Primary School

Happiness

Happiness is when someone comes to play.
Happiness is red and gold.
Happiness is Liverpool.
Happiness is a Liverpool strip.
Happiness is Steven Gerrard scoring a goal.
Happiness is Liverpool winning the European Cup.
Happiness is going to Anfield.
Happiness is the best thing ever.

Luke Hutchinson (8)
Newbottle Primary School

Red Is . . .

Red is a blazing fire,
Red is the petals of a rose,
Red is a car zooming past,
Red is the colour of a heart,
Red is a sunset setting in the sky.
Red is the pointer of the hour hand,
Red is the colour of a finish line banner,
Red is the breast of a robin,
Red is the colour of a file,
Red is a nice colour to look at,
Red is all around us.

Darren McCone (8)
Newbottle Primary School

A Good Time

A good time is when it's your birthday and you get loads of presents.
A good time is when you score the winning goal for your team.
A good time is when you go somewhere to play.
A good time is when you go outside and meet new friends.
A good time is when you come home from school and your favourite film is on.
A good time is when your mam goes out and brings something back for you.
A good time is when your best football team wins the FA Cup.
A good time is when you go to a special place.
A good time is when you go to the pictures with your friends.

James Robinson (8)
Newbottle Primary School

What Is It?

What is it?
It is the amazing sun
What is it?
It's the green tree
What is it?
It's the green grass
What is it?
It's a wild bull chasing the red Roman
What is it?
It is a big giant
What is it?
It is the flashing light
I can see at last.

Dominic Hogg (8)
Newbottle Primary School

My Gran

My gran is as mad as a bowling ball,
crashing down the aisles.
Her hair is as curly as a cow's tail,
sticking up.
Her eyes are like blue diamonds,
glistening in the light.
Her face looks like rocks,
crumpled on a cliff.
When she walks she is like a broom,
walking left and right.
When she sits she is like the Queen,
sitting on her royal chair.
When she laughs she is as giggly as a drink of pop,
fizzing out of the bottle.
When she sleeps she is as loud as pebbles,
smashing on the path.
The best thing about my gran is that she is as fun as a kitten,
playing in the garden.

Nicole Heslop (8)
Newbottle Primary School

My Gran

My gran is as sweet as a strawberry fresh from the field,
Her hair is as curly as a pig's tail and brown like mud,
Her eyes are like the blueness of the sea,
Her face is like a crumpled up piece of paper,
When she walks she is like a bride walking quickly down the aisle,
When she sits she is as proud as a peacock,
When she laughs she is like a witch casting a spell on someone,
When she sleeps she is as silent as a mouse,
The best thing about my gran is that she helps clean up my mess.

Katie Coyles (8)
Newbottle Primary School

Happiness is . . .

Happiness is waking up and smelling toast cooking,
Happiness is when my favourite football team win a match,
Happiness is when your parents take you to your favourite restaurant,
Happiness is when it is your birthday and you get loads of money,
Happiness is when you go to the shop and buy sweets,
Happiness is when you enjoy yourself at swimming,
Happiness goes in and out of your life.

Megan Parkinson (8)
Newbottle Primary School

What I Like To See

I like to see my mum waiting at the gate,
I like to see my friends playing happily,
I like to see the boys playing football all day,
I like to see our teacher every day,
I like to see the traffic lights and the cars go by,
I like to see the pop stars on the dazzling, colourful stage,
I like to see the waves go up and down in the deep blue sea,
I like to see everything.

Emily Krohn (8)
Newbottle Primary School

A Good Time

A good time is when it's your birthday,
A good time is when you're going somewhere special,
A good time is when your football team wins,
A good time is when you complete a game on your GameBoy,
A good time is when you get a new book,
A good time is when you watch TV,
A good time is when you get new Pokémon cards,
A good time is when you make new friends,
A good time is when you eat nice food,
A good time is just a nice way of life.

Joseph Dixon (8)
Newbottle Primary School

Happiness

Happiness is finding out it's Saturday,
Happiness is getting a surprise,
Happiness is when you see your family,
Happiness is watching whatever you want on TV,
Happiness is having an adventure,
Happiness is getting pocket money,
Happiness is playing with your friends,
Happiness is eating sweets,
Happiness is playing in the snow,
Happiness pops into your life when you least expect it.

Sophie Longford (9)
Newbottle Primary School

I Can See . . .

I can see the colourful rainbow stretching from one side to the other,
I can see the beautiful, clear blue sky,
I like to see horses running happily in a field,
I like to see my dog waiting for me in the house,
I like to see birds flying in the sky,
I love to see Newcastle United play football and win,
I like to see my friends and family,
I'm happy I can read,
I like to look at the big, puffy clouds and try to see pictures,
I really love seeing my dad and giving him a cuddle,
I love the world,
I'm glad I can see.

Olivia Highley (9)
Newbottle Primary School

Happiness

Happiness is when your friends are nice to you,
Happiness is when we get a class certificate,
Happiness is having fun,
Happiness is on your birthday,
Happiness is going to the swimming baths,
Happiness is playing games,
Happiness is playing in the snow with your friends,
Happiness is sleeping at my auntie's,
Happiness is when the sun shines so you can go outside,
Happiness is good.

Sarah Whittaker (9)
Newbottle Primary School

A Good Time Is . . .

A good time is when my favourite team wins,
A good time is when I go on a roller coaster,
A good time is when I sit in front of the TV,
A good time is when I go to my favourite shops,
A good time is when I play with my mate,
A good time is when I have a school dinner,
A good time is the best.

Cameron Williamson (9)
Newbottle Primary School

Happiness

Happiness is waking up and it is Saturday,
Happiness is going on a really good roller coaster,
Happiness is a sunny playtime,
Happiness is when your mam buys you your favourite book,
Happiness is getting on with your friends,
Happiness is when it snows and you can have fun,
Happiness is when you go on fun school trips,
Happiness is when you can play with others.
Happiness is fun!

Bethany Alexander (9)
Newbottle Primary School

What Makes A Supercar Super?

Ferrari looks, Bugatti speed
Are these the only things I need?

What about bling,
Is this the thing?

Furry dice,
They aren't so nice.

Loud exhaust,
Is annoying of course.

Alloy wheels coloured in blue,
Blacked-out windows, you can't see through.

Gull wing doors that open up wide,
Big racing stripes right down each side.

Sound system's blasting music out,
To talk in the car you'd have to shout.

A private reg with my name on
What would be better than Andaz1?

Turbo engines supercharged speed
How much horsepower would I need?

TVs and PlayStations in every headrest
This car would surely be the best.

If it had all this, it would be very dear,
It might even appear on Top Gear.

One day I'll drive this car somehow
But only in my dreams for now.

Andrew Taylor (10)
St Gregory's RC JMI Primary School, South Shields

Peace Begins To Fade

Achtung, achtung!
The Germans are invading
The year is 1939
And hopes of peace are fading.

Take cover, take cover!
The air raid warning sounds
People running to escape
In shelters underground.

Charge, charge!
Hitler is around
Bringing pain and misery
To all whom they surround.

Attack, attack!
The allies are succeeding
Towns won back, one by one,
The German line's receding.

Hooray, hooray!
The battle has been won
The year is 1945
The allies work is done.

Alexander Holt (9)
St Gregory's RC JMI Primary School, South Shields

The Magic Of Fairies

Where fairies spread their wings
And grant people's dreams,
The sparkles of magical things,
Shine like silver moonbeams.

They glide on the stripes of the rainbow
And dance every night on the stars,
Their wings glisten like white snow,
So bright you can see them on Mars.

Their wings glisten in the moonlight,
They have lips of rosebud-red,
They only come out at first light,
When most of us are tucked up in bed.

Anna Smith (8)
St Gregory's RC JMI Primary School, South Shields

My Dream Is . . .

My dream is . . .
To be a big star
and drive around in a fancy car.

My dream is . . .
To be a famous runner
and go diving in the summer.

My dream is . . .
To be a professional actress
and own my own doctor's practice.

My dream is . . .
To have a massive celebrity party
and get a black belt in karate.

My dream is . . .
To be an excellent artist
and be in a band as a guitarist.

My dream is . . .
To be a fashion designer
and take to the ocean on a liner.

For all the things I want to do and be
I'm so glad I'm *me!*

Emma Roberts (11)
St Gregory's RC JMI Primary School, South Shields

Blitz

Out and about there are no cars
All you can see are the bright stars
Sitting here in the dark
As I look out over the park
There goes the siren
The guns start firing
Down to the shelter we all go
Mum, me, Dad and Joe
No time to grab a coat or sweater
If I had I'd feel much better
Boom! Boom! Boom! I can hear the bombs
The planes must be over old Mr Tom's
You can feel the heat
From your head to your feet
Fire is near
It'll be a while for the all-clear
Boom! Boom! Boom! When will they stop?
Probably about 12 o'clock
We've been here for quite some hours
Sitting here under the flowers
I'm sitting here in my gown
Feeling sad and quite down
The bombers are heading away
They've done their work for today
Surely this month which is December
Will be a month to remember.

Laura Crutwell (10)
St Gregory's RC JMI Primary School, South Shields

What Would It Be Like?

What would it be like if we could fly way up high
With glorious wings, right up in the sky?
Without the need of planes at all
Life would be much different.

What would it be like if we could breathe under the sea
Befriending the sharks, not being their tea?
To swim where no one's swam before
Life would be much different.

What would it be like if gravity was no more?
We'd bounce around and float out through the door.
With no one keeping their feet on the ground
Life would be much different.

What would it be like if the world was made of sweets?
No one would go hungry; we'd always have treats
With constant sugar supply
Life would be much different.

What would it be like if animals could talk?
There would be no more barks, no neighs, no more squawks.
With most living things having the power of speech
Life would be much different.

Would it be much better?

Ellen Smith (11)
St Gregory's RC JMI Primary School, South Shields

If I Had A Baby Sister

If I had a baby sister
I'd have to change her nappy
I would play with her and read to her
And try to make her happy.

If I had a baby sister
I'd put her to sleep
I'd sing her favourite lullaby
Called, 'Bleat, Bleat, Bleat'.

If I had a baby sister
I'd take her for a walk
And my mum would say
On your way teach her how to talk.

If I had a baby sister
I would take her off to school
There she would learn right from wrong
And not to act like a fool.

If I had a baby sister
I'd wish she would be good
If she wasn't I would teach her
As much as I could.

If I had a baby sister
We would never be apart
I would always be there for her
I'd love her with all my heart.

Jade Richardson (8)
St Gregory's RC JMI Primary School, South Shields

Months Of The Year

January is a cold month, it makes me feel so blue.
February is about the same, I always catch the flu.
March is getting better, the nights are not so long.
April makes me happy, Easter bunnies and birds in song.
May might be a good month, depending on the wind.
June the sunshine's blazing and my winter clothes are binned.
July comes with great happiness, there's no more school for a while.
August brings the family holiday, that always makes me smile.
September's back to school again, so sad there's no more fun.
October's cold and winter's here, no more playing in the sun.
November brings excited cheer, for Christmas is on its way.
December is a lovely month, filled with love that's here to stay.

Amy Robinson (11)
St Gregory's RC JMI Primary School, South Shields

If I Had My Own Pony

If I had my own pony
I'd keep him in his stable
If I had my own pony
I'd visit him every hour
But only if I was able!

If I had my own pony
I think I'd call him Tony
If I had my own pony
I wouldn't let him be bony.

If I had my own pony
I'd feed him lots of hay
If I had my own pony
I'd feed him every day.

If I had my own pony
I'd go to the beach and paddle
If I had my own pony
I'd try not to fall off my saddle!

If I had my own pony
I would do lots of rise and trots
If I had my own pony
I would love him lots and lots and lots!

Kate Moss (7)
St Gregory's RC JMI Primary School, South Shields

The Galaxy

It's very dark up here in the sky,
We're up in a rocket, flying high
The sun is blinding
The moon looks cold
Mars is red, dusty and old.

Pluto is rather small
Venus is a pile of lava
I can't stay on my feet
Oh let's not bother, it's such a palaver.

Elinor Grant (9)
St Gregory's RC JMI Primary School, South Shields

What Shall I Be When I Grow Up?

What shall I be when I grow up?
Will I work in some fancy bars
Or maybe I will work in a garage repairing cars?
Shall I be a fancy illustrator
Or will I work in a restaurant as a waiter?

What shall I be when I grow up?
Will I work as a chief inspector
Or maybe I will work as a tax collector?
Shall I be an astronaut and fly around the universe
Or will I be a helping nurse?

What shall I be when I grow up?
Will I work as a successful plumber
Or maybe I will work in a band and be the drummer?
Shall I be a lifeguard watching al the people by the pool
Or will I be a teacher working in a school?

What shall I be when I grow up?
Will I work as a judge in court
Or maybe I will work in an airport?
Shall I be a lollipop lady and check that the roads are clear
Or will I be a hard-working engineer?

What shall I be when I grow up?
Will I work as an instructor who trains people how to be a scuba-diver
Or maybe I will work as a racing car driver?
Shall I be a singer and hit the chart list
Or will I be a famous artist?

What shall I be when I grow up?
Will I work in a shop and be a fantastic baker
Or maybe I will work as a dressmaker?
Shall I be an athlete and be first across the finish line
Or will I work in some dingy mine?

Holly Jackson (10)
St Gregory's RC JMI Primary School, South Shields

The World

Thank you for taking a little time
To read this little poem
About the giant planet Earth
Our one and only home.

When God created the solar system,
He found there was something missing,
So He decided to create a planet Earth,
With lots of love and kissing.

First He made the seas,
Vast areas of blue,
He made whales and seaweed
And lots of fish too!

Then He made the land
And filled it with animals,
His favourites of course,
Were all the lovely mammals.

Then He made the sky
And covered it with gleaming stars
And brought in lots and lots of birds
And gave us a view to nearby Mars.

At last the Earth was finished,
But was missing one thing,
Better than all the fish to swim,
Or all the birds to sing,
So God placed man and woman on the Earth,
He is our one true King.

Brendan Donnelly (11)
St Gregory's RC JMI Primary School, South Shields

My Brother

My brother, he's a really big lad,
In fact he's nearly as big as dad.

He likes karate, he loves to party,
His appetite is really hearty.

When not at school he sails and swims,
He has such fun, I want to join in.

My brother loves maths and books,
His computer skills bring envious looks,
If I am good and try to please,
I'll grow to be as nice as he is.

Rachael Donnelly (8)
St Gregory's RC JMI Primary School, South Shields

My Home Town

My home town means so much to me
It's special to me because it's near the sea
My family and friends all live nearby
If they lived far away I know I would cry.

It's nice to travel to different places
But it's nice to come home with my cases
To see the cliff tops and the beautiful beach
Then I know all the things I love are in reach.

There are boats and swans on the lake in the park
There is a pier and a lighthouse that shines in the dark
Do you know my home town, have you guessed?
It's called South Shields, the place that's the best.

Hannah Gibson (9)
St Gregory's RC JMI Primary School, South Shields

The Wind

The wind is so peaceful
The wind is so calm
It rustles through the trees
But does no harm.

It blows through my hair
On a blustery sunny day
When I'm on my swing
It takes the heat of the sun away.

The wind is so strong
Howling through the night
Clatters against the windowpane
On a cold, stormy night.

Leah Cowie (9)
St John Bosco School, Sunderland

The Lazy Dog

There is a lazy dog
He even has his own room.

All he has to do is lean over
And his food and drink will be there
He leans over to do everything.

He thinks the streets are his own
He never gets off the sofa
He wags his tail all over the room.

Shannon Carmody (9)
St John Bosco School, Sunderland

The Wild Child

I am a child
I am very wild
But don't blame me
'Cause you will see.

I went to my dad
Running very mad
My dad said to me,
'What did you see?'

I went to the park
And heard a dog bark
I sat on a swing
And found a bird's wing.

Chelsea Atkinson (10) & Ethan Turnbull (9)
St John Bosco School, Sunderland

St John Bosco

St John Bosco school is very cool
Everybody likes to go to school
Playing games, having such fun
Doing lessons in the sun.
Shirts, ties, black shoes too
School uniform is very cool.
In our hall there is lots to do,
So why don't you jump in our pool?
When you go out on a sunny day,
There are a lot of new and neat games to play.

Shannon Doughty & Katie Averre (9)
St John Bosco School, Sunderland

Work, Work, Work

I like to do English,
I like to do maths,
There are lots of different ways
And lots of different paths.

I like doing science,
It's OK,
We're learning the difference
Between night and day.

I like to do history,
I think it's fun.
We're learning about the war
And how it was won.

Courtney Snowball (10) & Stephanie Stewart (9)
St John Bosco School, Sunderland

Football

I play football all of the time
It's better than making up this rhyme.
I support my football team
And they're not as bad as they may seem.

Watching them on a weekend
Singing aloud as though it was a trend.
When I get back I am so wet
If we lose I lose my bet.

If we win the Carling Cup
It will be a dream come true
Just for me and just for you.

Jordon Dyer (10)
St John Bosco School, Sunderland

Teachers!

In my school there is a rule
Just beware of the teachers
There're small ones and tall ones
But in the hall there is the head of us all.

It's the head
She's very tall
With short brown hair
Just beware of the teachers!

What do they do when we're outside?
I think they put their slippers on
And dance around a child
But just beware of the teachers.

When it's dinnertime
We go down to the hall,
We're always last,
But the teachers they'll eat it all.

Kristie Smith (10)
St John Bosco School, Sunderland

My Pet Is . . .

My pet is small and grey,
But my pet doesn't live in the hay.
My pet lives in a cage,
But my pet is not called Paige.

My pet is a hamster,
But my pet is not a prancer.
My pet runs behind the cooker,
I wonder if he does play snooker?

My pet's name begins with C
But he is not a bumblebee
Because he is called Chippie.

Sophie-Lea Humphries (10)
St John Bosco School, Sunderland

What Is . . . Snow?

Snow is a drifting cloud,
Shredded like a piece of paper.

Snow is cornflakes, covered in snow,
Hitting the ground like feathers.

Snow is on trees glistening and sparkling,
Thin, it is falling gracefully.

Isabelle Jackson (10)
St Mary's RC Primary School, Sunderland

What Is . . . The Snow?

It is a cloud of soft white snow in the air.
It is a leaf for a tree in the blue sky.
It is a white snow blanket for a cold path.
It is a white snow puddle lying on the floor.
It is an igloo made out of soft white snow.

Harriet Behan (9)
St Mary's RC Primary School, Sunderland

Puppy - Haiku

It has its eyes closed
It is so adorable
So please be quiet!

Robert Winlow (9)
St Mary's RC Primary School, Sunderland

Flower

Flower blossoming, blooming bright
To catch the sunlight but not the night
Water succulent on rainy days
Sucked up the stalk till sunlight fades.

Hannah Trotter (10)
St Mary's RC Primary School, Sunderland

Butterfly

Tiny orb underneath leaf
Patiently waiting until . . .
Crack, out comes the larva
Like a snake shedding its skin
While gnawing and eating everything green.
Spinning and winding silken thread
Turning into a chrysalis, sleeping in his bed
Changing in his deep sleep
Emerging from the chrysalis
The butterfly spreads his wings and off he flies.

Jack Hindmarch (10)
St Mary's RC Primary School, Sunderland

Hallowe'en

Hallowe'en is coming soon,
In the sky there will be a full moon,
Scary skeletons and ghastly ghosts
They're the ones that scare you the most
Reading about red devils and bats
And seeing all the witches' hats
Knocking on the neighbours' doors
And standing on the creaking floors
Witches on broomsticks flying through the night
They might jump out and give you a fright
Sweets and treats for all to share
Come to my house, if you dare.

Christopher Hutcheon (10)
St Mary's RC Primary School, Sunderland

Sunderland

Saturday afternoon we go to the game
It doesn't matter if it's sunshine or rain.
Sunderland AFC is our team
Winning the Premiership is our dream
Gradually the players are playing together
Julio Arca is our star player
He makes a defender shake with fear
Premiership we're here
So come on Sunderland win today.

Clayton Atkinson (10)
St Mary's RC Primary School, Sunderland

Fairies

Fairies are pretty,
Magic and witty.
They dash outside,
With lots of pride.
And all around,
The nice clean ground.

They spread their dust,
As if they must.
They shall go home for tea,
With no car or key.
Then go up to bed
With their sleepy little head.

Then await for the light,
To enter the night.
And eat something sour
To load up their power.

Caroline Barker (10)
St Mary's RC Primary School, Sunderland

Sunderland

At night the black cats get ready to play
The stadium is like Heaven
Go and get your hot dog before they start
When they win
Even the fish flap their fins
Red and white, roar!

Joseph Alder (9)
St Mary's RC Primary School, Sunderland

Blue Whale

Blue is his colour
He swims through the sea
His tail a jackhammer
Eating krill all day
And swimming
But in the distance
The hunter is coming.

Nicholas Atkinson (10)
St Mary's RC Primary School, Sunderland

Butterflies

Fluttering in the air,
All different colours from the wings
Transformation from a caterpillar,
Gentle, placid creatures,
Wings wafer-thin,
Legs as light as air,
Live on . . . we don't know
Very fast to catch,
Moths and dragonflies,
Related to the
Butterfly.

Victoria Measham (9)
St Mary's RC Primary School, Sunderland

Dolphin

In and out the water
Splish and splash
Come for a ride
On my slide.

We have magic underground
Meet my babies in the sea
It is great, just wait and see.

Eleanor Stout (10)
St Mary's RC Primary School, Sunderland

What Is Ice?

Ice is like glass
See-through and cold.

Ice is a model
Carved and kept safe.

Ice is defeated
By the burning-hot sun.

Ice is like a crystal
Coloured and bought.

Ice of a ring
On sale for women.

Matthew Johnson (10)
St Mary's RC Primary School, Sunderland

What Is . . . Wind?

Wind is a giant whistling up above
Wind is rustling trees who have no form of defence
Wind is unstoppable no matter how many times you try
Wind is a helper, to help you when you call
Stay with us wind, glorious wind stay forever!

Charlotte Robson (9)
St Mary's RC Primary School, Sunderland

What Is . . . Snow?

Snow is fur on a polar bear's back
It is a sparkling carpet under the street lamp
It is a piece of crinkled up paper
It is a ruler broken up
It is a whiteboard taken to pieces.

Lloyd Purvis (9)
St Mary's RC Primary School, Sunderland

What Are . . . Clouds?

The clouds are cotton wool floating in the summer sky
It's an angel's dress bouncing up and down
It's a white cushion jumping around in the sky
It's a fluffy coat dancing around happily
It's a blanket drifting around in the sky.

Mary Querry (9)
St Mary's RC Primary School, Sunderland

What Are Clouds?

Clouds are like puffed up pillows that are floating in the air
Clouds are like cuddly blankets for when you are very cold
Clouds are like smiley faces smiling back at you!

Alice Fairweather (9)
St Mary's RC Primary School, Sunderland

What Is Ice?

Ice is like an ice rink shining in the floodlights
Ice is like a slippery carpet under a street light
Ice is like a diamond hanging in the gutter
Ice is like an iceberg floating in the frozen sea
Ice is clear as crystal under a patch of frozen water.

Thomas Bates (9)
St Mary's RC Primary School, Sunderland

What Is . . . Snow?

Snow is shredded up cloud, cut with the horn of a rhino
It is a stampede of ghosts forming to make a crystal carpet
It is feathers off an angel's wings to make a pale white blanket
It is sheep's wool from an eight-armed sheep falling from
the planet Uranus
It is particles of sweet sugar on a giant Christmas cake.

Adam Szandrowski (9)
St Mary's RC Primary School, Sunderland

What Is Ice?

What is ice?
Dazzling blue sea frozen solid in the icy cold tomb
Ice does not come in the summer, it comes in winter
The best place to find ice is Antarctica.

Brendan Murray (9)
St Mary's RC Primary School, Sunderland

What Is A Rainbow?

A rainbow is a colourful umbrella high in the sky
Drifting round corners you turn.

The more you turn, the more colourful you get
The pot of gold you have just met.

When you run it spreads in the air
Just to make the world look fair.

Chantelle Richardson (9)
St Mary's RC Primary School, Sunderland

What Is . . . Wind?

Wind is air - the kind that sweeps through your hair
It is a gust, the gust that you never trust
Wind is strong, it can blow so long
Wind can blow down a tree and you and me.

Ethan Cubby (9)
St Mary's RC Primary School, Sunderland

Spider - Haiku

Spiders hunt for prey -
Through the night and through the day . . .
Then they stop and feast!

Jamie Carmody (10)
St Mary's RC Primary School, Sunderland

Moonlight

The moon is a baboon dancing to a tune
In the spotlight doing a twirl and a swirl
Moving here and there
Lighting up the world.

Alex Brook (9)
St Mary's RC Primary School, Sunderland

In The Coal Mine

In the bleak, dark and dull mine
More dangerous than a beehive
You work at the age of 9 to 12
When you're smaller than little elves
You push a cart filled with coal
Till you get to scraping out your bowl
We work twelve hours a day
We come back dead and cannot play.

Daniel Harrison (9)
St Mary's RC Primary School, Sunderland

Beserker

Red is their colour
They are reborn from mud
They kill with their double-sided sword
To serve the white wizard Saruman.

Lewis Meldrum (9)
St Mary's RC Primary School, Sunderland

River Of Red Devils

Red Devils all around
Striking people with the ball
Scoring goals in sight
Setting balls alight
All you see is a river of fire
People scream with joy and happiness
They take the winning cup home
And live with it forever.

Lewis Lonsdale (9)
St Mary's RC Primary School, Sunderland

Harvest Poem

Juicy strawberries
Watery melons
Sweet pears
Bright oranges
Green lettuce
Juicy bananas
Round potatoes.

Wayne Wilkinson (12)
Trinity Kenton Lodge (EBD Special School)

Harvest Poem

Ripening strawberries
Sweet red apples
Deafening harvester
Cold frosty windows
Ice on car windows
Snow on the roof
Sleet on the roads.

Robert Neailey (12)
Trinity Kenton Lodge (EBD Special School)

Harvest Poem

Cold air,
Rusty coloured leaves,
Delicious fruit,
Fresh, tasty vegetables,
Warm cosy fire,
Hardworking farmers,
Animals hibernate,
Sun rises late.

Karl Johnston (12)
Trinity Kenton Lodge (EBD Special School)

Harvest Poem

Succulent oranges,
Tasty pears,
Ripened bananas,
Juicy apples,
Mashed potatoes,
Crunchy carrots
And seedy tomatoes.

Jack Auty (12)
Trinity Kenton Lodge (EBD Special School)

Tell Me Please

'Tell me, tell me, tell me please,
Who on earth likes mouldy peas?'
How about Leon?
Not Leon
Leon likes lions
Leon likes long walks
Leon likes lessons
Leon likes letters.

Leon Dunkerley (12)
Trinity Kenton Lodge (EBD Special School)

Tell Me Please

'Tell me, tell me, tell me please,
Who on earth likes buzzing bees?'
How about Kirsty?
Not Kirsty!
Kirsty likes kittens
Kirsty likes koala bears
Kirsty likes kisses
Kirsty likes cooking.

Kirsty Smith (13)
Trinity Kenton Lodge (EBD Special School)

Harvest Poem

Juicy apples
Smoky breath
Delicious fruit
Red berries
Blue sky
Frosty mornings
Fresh air
Trees bare.

Joe Cooper (12)
Trinity Kenton Lodge (EBD Special School)

Harvest Poem

Animals hibernate
Juicy fruit
Green vegetables
Farmers' crops
Fresh bread
Spiders' webs
Morning sunrise
Late sunset
Bright hot fire.

Zoe Ankers (12)
Trinity Kenton Lodge (EBD Special School)

Harvest Poem

Frosty breath
Noisy harvester
Animals hibernating
Fresh fruit
Half of a spider's web
Juicy red berries
Smoky breath.

Andy Gordon (11)
Trinity Kenton Lodge (EBD Special School)

Tell Me Please

'Tell me, tell me, tell me please,
Who on earth likes knobbly knees?'
How about Kayleigh?
Not Kayleigh!
Kayleigh likes kittens
Knitting, clowns, koala bears
Computer games, cuddles.

Kayleigh Corby (13)
Trinity Kenton Lodge (EBD Special School)

One Two, Three, What Can I See?

One, two, three
What can I see?
The chubby, huge elephant
Throwing his peanuts at me.

A, B, C
What can I see?
My 6-week-old puppy
Looking at me.

Abbie Pollard (10)
Trinity Kenton Lodge (EBD Special School)

Tell Me Please

'Tell me, tell me, tell me please,
Who on earth likes smelly cheese?'
How about Kyle?
Not Kyle!
Kyle likes koala bears
Kyle likes cakes
Kyle likes kites
Kyle likes kebabs.

Kyle Smith (11)
Trinity Kenton Lodge (EBD Special School)

Lots Of Things

One train but lots of trains
One wish but lots of wishes
One chair but lots of chairs
And one hat but lots of hats.

One fox but lots of foxes
One pen but lots of pens
One glass but lots of glasses
And one flash but lots of flashes.

One church but lots of churches
One light but lots of lighters
One bird but lots of birds
One match but lots of matches
And one catch but lots of catches.

Brian Parker (12)
Trinity Kenton Lodge (EBD Special School)

The Stunt Park

I go to the stunt park
Along with my friends.
When it starts to get dark
We pedal off and go home.

David Lavery (11)
Trinity Kenton Lodge (EBD Special School)

My Telly

When I go home from school,
I rush to watch my telly,
It is big and wide,
Just like my grandad's belly!

Billy Ray Rose (11)
Trinity Kenton Lodge (EBD Special School)

Fantasy Fibs

I saw a fat, ugly tooth fairy
Eating lollipops and popcorn
She looked very scary
Sitting on my lawn
No you never, you never
I did!

Carl Woods (11)
Trinity Kenton Lodge (EBD Special School)

Fantasy Fibs

I saw Batman
Tap-dancing in space
With his frying pan
And vanity case
No you never, you never
I did!

David Stewart (12)
Trinity Kenton Lodge (EBD Special School)

Fantasy Fibs

I saw Santa Claus beating up a boy
With a baseball bat -
I saw him playing with a toy
And strangling a cat
No you never, you never
I did!

Jacob Harvey (12)
Trinity Kenton Lodge (EBD Special School)

Tell Me Please

'Tell me, tell me, tell me please,
Who on earth likes jumping fleas?'
How about Johnathon?
Not Johnathon!
Johnathon likes jelly, juggling,
Jelly beans and jam.

Johnathon Cameron (12)
Trinity Kenton Lodge (EBD Special School)

The Hilltop

Standing on the hilltop
Gazing at the grass
As beautiful as
Diamonds
And
Glamorous
As glass.

Chellsie Lee Hall (10) & Amy Robson (9)
Wharrier Street Primary School

Treats

I love ice cream,
I love sweets,
I love all kinds of treats.
When it comes to bedtime,
Mum tells me to go upstairs and clean my teeth.

Lauren Lister (10)
Wharrier Street Primary School

The Key

In a world there is a country,
In a country there is a city,
In the city there is a town,
In the town there is a street,
In the street there is a house,
In the house there is a room,
In that room there is a bed,
On the bed there is a key
And that key opens your dream box
And in the dream box there is . . . ?

Connor Taylor (9)
Wharrier Street Primary School

Friends Don't Quit

Friends don't quit even at bad times
So dry your eyes
To get a big surprise
That friends don't quit
Especially special friends
So dry your eyes
To get a big surprise
My best friend.

Rachael Langley (9)
Wharrier Street Primary School